THEN AND TH...

GENERAL EDITOR

MARJORIE REEVES, M.A., Ph.D.

Railway Revolution

1825-1845

MARJORIE GREENWOOD, M.A.

Illustrated from contemporary sources by

S. GREENWOOD

LONGMAN

LONGMAN GROUP LIMITED
London

*Associated companies, branches and representatives
throughout the world*

*First published 1955
Thirteenth impression 1974*

ISBN 0 582 20382 1

The drawing on page 43 is redrawn from the cover of
G.F. Westcott's *The British Railway Locomotive 1803-1853*,
by permission of the Controller of H.M. Stationery Office.

*Printed in Hong Kong by
Sheck Wah Tong Printing Press*

CONTENTS

TO THE READER

EVERY fact in this book comes from some record written at the time the book is describing; nothing has been invented in these pages, which seek to be a true record of the life and thought of people who themselves planned and made and travelled on the first railways. What they wrote are original sources to which historians have to go back for their information. You will find out more about these original sources by reading pages 35 and 36. If you want to write a historical play or novel, see if you too can take all your detail exactly and accurately from original sources.

In the same way all the pictures in this book are based on a drawing made by someone who lived then and there.

By studying what people said in word and picture about themselves, you will come to feel at home in one ' patch ' of the history of the past and really live with the group of people as they thought and worked then and there. And gradually you will be able to fill in more patches of history.

THIS book is about transport in 1845, that is, how goods and people moved about England more than 100 years ago. You will remember that, at the end of the eighteenth century and the beginning of the nineteenth, there were new machines and new ways of making things—a change which is called the Industrial Revolution. There were also changes in transport so that by 1845 ways of moving things were different from what they had been in 1760.

You will all have talked about what you are going to be when you leave school and some of you will already have it planned. Have you thought of being an engine driver? In 1845, a fourteen-year-old boy, James M'Connel, thought the most exciting job of all was to be a railway engineer, a man who actually built railways, who decided where the lines should be laid and where the stations should be built. Perhaps you would not have thought of THAT job, because, having so many railways in England to-day, we do not build many new ones. But in the England of 1845, when James was a boy, new lines were being planned and built in every direction. Indeed, so many lines were planned in that year, and so many people were talking and thinking about railway building, that we often call it 'the Year of the Railway Mania.' You will understand why later.

1

Of course, railways were not invented in 1845; the FIRST PUBLIC RAILWAY was opened between Stockton and Darlington in 1825. This was not the first time a locomotive drawing trucks had run on rails, as you will find out later, but it was the first PUBLIC railway. By 1845, hundreds of miles of public railways had been built.

We can learn about the early days of railways if we visit James M'Connel, who in 1845 was staying with his grandparents at Ardwick Hall, Manchester. You will understand later that James was very lucky in being able to find out so much for himself about railways. But first just a word about Manchester at that time.

To-day Manchester is one of the largest areas of houses and factories in this country. In every direction the original town of Manchester has joined with the towns and villages around it until it forms one huge mass of buildings and there are very few open spaces. In 1845, however, there were fields around the smaller town and Ardwick Hall was on the edge of it. The house was built in the time before the railways.

Like James himself, you will be wanting to hear about the early railways. So let us hear what James's grandfather, Mr. Kennedy, has to say about himself, for it will show you something of how railways came to be built. To-day when a new aeroplane flies it is because clever designers and civil engineers have worked together to make it, but you will see that this was not so in 1845 when a new railway line was opened. The odd thing about Mr. Kennedy, you may think, is that, although he was one of the men who planned the first railway from Manchester, he was not an expert in the making of roads or canals. He was a cotton manufacturer. You will learn in the story how he came to plan the railway.

JOHN KENNEDY TELLS HOW THE LIVERPOOL AND MANCHESTER RAILWAY WAS BUILT

James was waiting impatiently for his grandfather in the drawing-room of Ardwick Hall. He knew that his grandfather had been to a very important meeting that afternoon about the railway and he wanted to ask all about it. Indeed, his grandfather had promised to tell him when he returned. He was looking at the book which his Uncle John had given him for Christmas, when his grandmother, Mrs. Kennedy, spoke to him.

"James, stop turning over the pages of that book! Choose one page and read from it."

"But, Grandmother, I must turn over the pages of THIS book to find what I want."

"What is the book then?"

"It is the RAILWAY COMPANION, Grandmother, and I am trying to find out how long it takes to travel to London."

"Always railways, railways, railways! James, why can't you read another book?"

"Oh no, Mother," said Uncle John, "let the boy read Bradshaw, if he wants to."

"Wasting his time, I call it," said Mrs. Kennedy.

"Hardly that, Mamma. Everyone ought to be able to find out train times to-day. Can you find the time of my train to-morrow in your guide, James? I am going to Liverpool in the morning and hope to finish my business there about two o'clock."

"Oh yes, Uncle, I think so. Yes, here it is."

(You will find what James was looking at on page 78.)

"The train in the morning, Uncle, goes at 9 o'clock and there is a first-class one back at 4.15 p.m."

3

"What time does the train reach Manchester, James, for we shall want to know when to send the carriage?" said Aunt Eliza, who was Uncle John's wife.

"It does not say that; only the time it leaves Liverpool," replied James.

"Oh no, Eliza," laughed Uncle John, "Mr. Bradshaw knows better than to put in the time of arrival. There might be a cow on the line!"

"Oh, the poor creature!" said old Mrs. Kennedy.

"It doesn't often happen, Mother," said Uncle John, "not now that strong wooden fences are being put up along the line. So one day Mr. Bradshaw may be able to print the time of arrival of the trains."

The North-Western Railway Company is Formed

At this moment a fine horse pulled a carriage up the drive of Ardwick Hall, and James's grandfather came in. When he was settled by the fire, James said:

"I am glad that you have come home, Grandfather. Please tell me about your meeting this afternoon."

"It wasn't very exciting, James; just a lot of men sitting around a table signing papers. All the talking was done weeks ago. To-day the chief *shareholders*[1] of the Grand Junction Railway came to meet us of the Liverpool and Manchester Railway. We have agreed to join our two railways together and call them in future the North-Western Railway. This was all set out on pieces of paper which we signed this afternoon. By signing these papers we have put the railways of this part of England under one management. But I was just thinking, James, that this meeting this afternoon was not as exciting as the one I went to in 1824 in Liverpool."

"What did you do there, Grandfather?"

"Oh, that is where it all began. That's where we planned the first railway in this district."

"Will you tell me about that meeting?"

James had heard much of it before, but he loved hearing his grandfather talking about the past. Mr. Kennedy liked telling his grandson, so he began:

"It was because I was a cotton manufacturer that I was interested in transport and there were many others who thought as I did. Do you know from where we get our raw cotton, James?"

"From America, Grandfather, don't you? It comes in ships to Liverpool and then by train to Manchester."

[1] You will find words printed like *this* in the Glossary on pages 91 and 92.

"That is right to-day; but this is 1845! What happened before 1830, in the days when there was no railway?"

"Oh, I see what you mean, Grandfather. There wasn't any way of getting it there."

"Yes, there was. At first the bales of cotton had come on packhorses and in wagons but the roads were so bad that men had built canals and deepened the River Mersey. That was fifty years ago; but the boats were small and as we built more machinery and drove it by steam, we wanted more cotton from Liverpool. There were four ways of getting it to Manchester in 1820, as you see on this map.

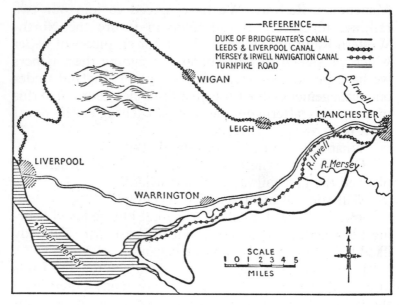

"The *turnpike* road had been repaired but not many bales of cotton could be loaded on one cart and it took a whole day on the journey. More bales of cotton could travel in a barge on the rivers and canals than in a wagon

6

but they took days on the journey and sometimes weeks. Why! men said that it took longer to move a bale of cotton from Liverpool to Manchester than it took the boat to cross the Atlantic Ocean, but perhaps that was an exaggeration.

"You must not think that we just decided to build the railway, James," his grandfather continued. "When I think of all the bother we had to get the Liverpool-Manchester line built, I wonder how we did it! You can't understand to-day, when we take the railways for granted, how different it was in 1824 when we started."

"Surely everyone wanted the railways to be built?" said James in a surprised voice.

"Indeed they did not," laughed Mr. Kennedy. "There was a great deal of opposition."

(Can you think of any reasons why people tried to stop the building of a railway? You will find other reasons, besides those mentioned by Mr. Kennedy, on page 80.)

"You must understand," Mr. Kennedy went on, "that a railway must run as straight as possible, otherwise it will not save time. So it will run over land belonging to many different men and you have to persuade them all to sell a strip of land to the railway company.

"As one man, by refusing to sell, could stop the whole line from being built, we had to have powers to force everyone to sell as we wanted. The only way of forcing them was by getting an Act passed by Parliament giving us this power. We also wanted to be able to pass over private land with our tools and machinery, for the railway was often some way from the roads. Now it costs money to get an Act through Parliament, so on May 24th, 1824, those of us who were interested in the scheme held a meeting to decide how we could collect the money."

"I can well remember that meeting," said Mr. Kennedy. "There were several men who later became famous, but on that day our only thought was to float this company and get our railway built. Everyone was tired of the hold the canals had over our business and wanted to end it."

"What do you mean by 'float a company'?" asked James.

"Oh, John, you do use odd words for the lad to understand," said Mrs. Kennedy.

"No, my dear," replied Mr. Kennedy. "The lad is growing up and must learn these affairs, even if he is only going to drive an engine and not manage his father's factory!

"Floating a company, James, means that we were starting one. I suppose that it comes from the days when several men would arrange at a meeting to pay for the building and equipping of a ship, and then they would share the profits. That was just what we were doing. We thought that we would need £300,000 to get our Act through Parliament and build our railway; so we split it into 3,000 lots of £100 each (or *shares* as they are called). Do you understand that if 3,000 men each put £100 into our scheme, we would have our money? Then later, the men who had put their money into our company would share the profits, which we hoped our railway would earn when it started to run. Of course, some men put more than £100 into the company, so we did not have 3,000 men with shares (or shareholders as they are called)."

"And did you have some shares, Grandfather?" asked James.

8

"Oh yes, I did. As some of us came from Manchester and some from Liverpool, we set some shares apart for men from these places, and the rest for the land-owners along the route. We hoped that they would be more likely to sell their land if they thought that they might earn money in the future by doing so."

"So that is what you did at the meeting, Grandfather?"

"Yes. We also drew up a *Prospectus*, or list of advantages of our railway line. We hoped with this to encourage men to lend us their money by showing them how quickly they might get a share of the profits.

"And, as I have already told you, we were hoping to cut out the canals. So we listed the four ways in which the railway would be better than the canals. Like this:

1. The railway will be 33 miles shorter than the canal.
2. The journey between Liverpool and Manchester will take between 4 and 5 hours, whereas by canal it takes at least 36 hours.
3. We are offering to the merchants of either town a regular service which will run every day and their goods will not be delayed by ice in winter and low water in summer as they have been on the canal.
4. We are offering to carry goods one-third cheaper than by the canal.

"And you made it sound very attractive, I'm sure," laughed Uncle John.

"Of course," replied Mr. Kennedy, "But then, it WAS attractive. We had Share Certificates printed to show how much money each man had invested in the company, and very nice they looked too, with a picture of Britannia on the top pointing to her railways."

There is a picture of one on the next page.

A Share Certificate

"What about the branch lines, Father?" said Uncle John. "Tell him about them."

"You planned branch lines even then?" asked Aunt Eliza.

"Oh yes. Most of us could see that one day there would be railway lines running in all directions across the country. Besides, there were places not far from our line between Manchester and Liverpool, like Bolton and St. Helens, which had goods to send away."

"Why ever those places, Father?" laughed Aunt Eliza.

"Good gracious, Eliza, don't you remember that they had recently opened up coal mining at St. Helens? And Bolton was already becoming a centre of cotton spinning and needed raw cotton brought by some other means than packhorses. There were many farmers too who, we hoped, would buy lime and manure and carry it on our trains. Then, too, we hoped to carry people as in a stage coach."

"I thought that was why trains ran," said James, "—to carry people."

"Oh no," replied Mr. Kennedy. "The Stockton and Darlington line was built only for goods but WE planned some trucks for people, though no one expected quite so many people to use them!"

(Have you noticed that Mr. Kennedy talks of 'trucks' for the people? If you look at the pictures of the early carriages on pages 60–61, you will see that they are very different from those you have travelled on.)

"So you have always carried passengers, Grandfather?"

"Yes, in the early years, to our surprise, we had more money from the passengers than from the goods! And during the first weeks, we could not carry any goods at all, there were so many people wanting to ride in the trains! There were plenty of visitors to see our railway. Many of them were men who were thinking of starting a line in their own district."

(If you wish to know some of the things said by these people about the Liverpool and Manchester Railway when their Acts were being examined by Parliament, you will find them on page 84.)

"So we planned our track of rails," continued Mr. Kennedy, "and the trucks to carry the goods. But how were the trucks to be drawn? That was not yet settled."

"But you would have a steam engine," said James.

"No, you must not think that all of us had thought that a steam engine would pull the trucks. I did, because I was something of an engineer, and besides, I knew James Watt and had heard of the early experiments which had been carried on."

"But what did the others think would draw the trucks?" asked James in a puzzled voice.

"They thought of laying rails, and then letting horses pull the trucks along! This had already been done for carrying coal in many parts of England."

"But you did have steam engines, Grandfather?" said James worriedly.

"We managed to persuade the others before the line was finished. Four of us, Sandar, Ellis, Booth and myself, went to see the Stockton to Darlington Railway. We saw steam engines working there, so we persuaded the others to let George Stephenson act as our engineer. We told how we had travelled in a truck at ten miles an hour."

(If you wish to know more about the early use of trucks running on rails for carrying coal, you will find it on page 37.)

"When we had drawn up our plans," continued Mr. Kennedy, "we began to receive money. The next step was to get the line *surveyed* and send the draft of our Act to Parliament. That wasn't easy either!

"We did all we could to try to hurry up the building of the line, but there were many people who did not want it. We knew from the beginning that we could not take the most direct route, for the Duke of Rutland refused to sell his land and a great landowner like that was not to be tempted with a few shares in our company. Some people, on the other hand, thought that they might make some money by having the railway pass over their land. They even tried to bribe Stephenson or his assistant Gooch to get the railway over their land and not in a direct line. Some wouldn't have Stephenson on their land to do the surveying."

"Oh yes," said Uncle John, "I can remember Mr. Stephenson telling us about his surveying adventures. He said that in one place he was driven off by gamekeepers, and in another the farmers had armed their labourers with picks and spades to stop him."

"So he couldn't make the survey?" asked James.

"Yes, he worked by moonlight when they were all in bed. He said that he needed only to walk over the land measuring and recording in his notebook and this he said he could do very well by the light of the moon."

"Mr. Stephenson is a very clever man," said Mr. Kennedy; "but, do you know, he finds writing and reading difficult. He always had Thomas Gooch with him to do the writing. I'll tell you more about him another time, but now let me go on with the story of the railway."

(You will find more about Stephenson on page 36.)

In Parliament

"At last the survey was made," Mr. Kennedy went on, "the plan of the line drawn out, the reasons for building the line written down and the Liverpool and Manchester Railroad *Bill* presented to Parliament. That began another struggle, for there were many men in Parliament who did not want the Bill. Many more had been persuaded to vote against it by our enemies outside the House. Some very strange reasons against it were put forward: the hens would stop laying, the cows grazing; the air would poison the birds, and the roofs of the houses near the line would be burnt. We were able, however, to prove that the methods of carrying goods between the two towns were poor, but it was a difficult thing to prove that a railroad was the best way of solving the problem. At the *Committee Stage*, our opponents argued every line and thirty-six days were taken up with it in 1825. One of our main supporters was poor Mr. Huskisson of Liverpool."

"Why 'poor', Grandfather?" asked James.

"He, poor man, was killed by one of the engines on the opening day, but I will tell you about that later. In 1825, he spoke many times on our behalf, but the Bill was rejected. We were so determined to have our railway that we sent the Bill up again the next year. That cost us a lot more money. I believe £70,000 was spent on getting the Bill through Parliament. At last we were successful and work could begin building the line.

"But that did not finish the difficulties for Mr. Stephenson! You know that the line had to be on the flat all the way. Now this had been easy between Stockton and Darlington, but the way between Liverpool and Manchester was uphill and down, and it all had to be made level.

The Olive Mount Cutting at Edge Hill, near Liverpool

"There were three main difficulties facing Mr. Stephenson: the higher ground at Edge Hill near Liverpool, the valley of the River Sankey, and Chat Moss near Manchester. I have some pictures of these which will show you what Mr. Stephenson had to solve. Please, John, the bundle in the third drawer of my desk."

When the bundle of pictures had been brought, Mr. Kennedy said, "This one is the Olive Mount Cutting at Edge Hill near Liverpool. The land was dug away for over two miles and it was a hundred feet deep in places." In the picture on the previous page you can see the men still taking the rock away as one of the first engines comes through. Can you imagine how much earth had to be dug out? When you next go through a *cutting*, remember the

The Viaduct across the Sankey Valley

16

only way then of getting the earth out was with picks and spades. Next we come to the Sankey Valley across which Mr. Stephenson built a *viaduct* on nine arches to keep the line level. It was built of brick with stone facings and was 70 feet above the water in the centre. How the railways changed the appearance of the countryside!

"Finally, nearer to Manchester was Chat Moss which many thought would stop the line being built."

"Chat Moss? What a strange name!" said James.

"'Moss' is a word they use in Lancashire to describe a swamp or marsh. Our enemies said that it couldn't be crossed. One engineer said: 'No engineer in his senses would go through Chat Moss. A railway cannot be safely made over it without going to the bottom.' It is a strange piece of country shaped like a saucer, so that all the water runs towards the centre. It is filled with dead moss which has gathered for many thousands of years with living moss on the top. It is like a great sponge which swells with water in wet weather. It was far too big to be drained and a viaduct across it would have been too costly.

"I am told that Daniel Defoe, who travelled near it a hundred years ago, said that 'the surface at a distance looks black and dirty, and is indeed frightful to think of, for it will bear neither horse nor man.' As no man could stand on it without sinking, everyone said it was silly for Stephenson to try to build a railway over it. However, Mr. Stephenson followed the example of John Metcalf, the Yorkshire road maker. He laid hurdles interwoven with heather to form a floating road. The men and horses of the district could walk over it with boards strapped to their feet (like snowshoes) because their weight was spread over a greater area. Mr. Stephenson made the floating road wider than the usual railway track. On this foundation he laid a thin layer of gravel, then sleepers, and rails, so that a train could be carried."

"And did you see the line being made, Grandfather?" asked James.

"Why yes, my lad. You remember too, don't you, John," he said, turning to his son, "how we used to walk down Liverpool Road and watch them digging and track-laying when the railway came near Manchester?"

"Of course I do, Father. I was about the same age as young James here and I used to spend most of my spare time down at the railway station. Do you know, James, that there were many hundreds of men working at once on the line, digging out the earth, filling wheelbarrows, wheeling them away, laying the rails, building walls and bridges?"

(You will find more detail and pictures of building a railway line before 1850 on page 62.)

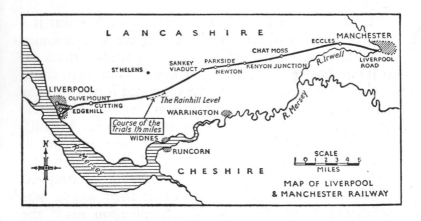

MAP OF LIVERPOOL
& MANCHESTER RAILWAY

"We still had not made up our minds at the beginning of 1829 how our trucks were to be drawn," continued Mr. Kennedy.

"I thought you had Mr. Stephenson's ROCKET, Grandfather?"

"Oh no, not at the beginning. We had Mr. Stephenson as our engineer to build the line, but not all the members of our committee were sure that his engine was the best. Most of us were quite sure that some *locomotive* was best, but we knew that other men besides Stephenson were making them. Some of the committee even thought that a *stationary engine* was better. They planned to have twenty-one of them built along the line, each of which would pull the train along by means of ropes as far as itself and then the train would hook on to the ropes of the next engine."

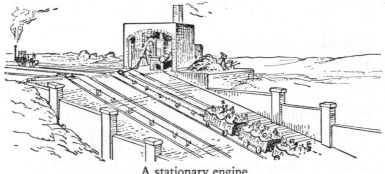

A stationary engine

"What a funny thing!"

"It may seem so to you, but they were used quite a lot in the collieries. We knew that it would be expensive to change later so we wanted the very best we could get at first. We decided to hold a competition to find the best way of drawing our trucks. We knew what the stationary engines could do, so we invited engineers to bring their steam engines to a finished part of our track at Rainhill and there we could see which was the best. I think I have the advertisement in this bundle of pictures. Yes, here it is in THE LIVERPOOL MERCURY for May 1st, 1829."

TO ENGINEERS AND IRON FOUNDERS

The Directors of the Liverpool and Manchester Railway hereby offer a premium of £500 (over and above the cost price) for a Locomotive Engine, which shall be a decided improvement on any hitherto constructed, subject to certain stipulations and conditions a copy of which may be had at the Railway office, or will be forwarded as may be directed, on application for the same, if by letter, post paid.

Henry Booth,
Treasurer.

Railway Office, Liverpool, April 25, 1829.

"You will notice, James," Mr. Kennedy continued, "that we wanted a locomotive which was better than any in existence, 'A decided improvement' we put in the advertisement. We wanted one which was faster, pulled more trucks and which did not weigh so much itself. We knew that we were making it very hard for the engineers, but then we offered a prize of £500, and we hoped we would get a really good engine, and we did. We got the ROCKET!

"But let us look at these pictures of the steam engines which were entered for the competition before I tell you more about the trials."

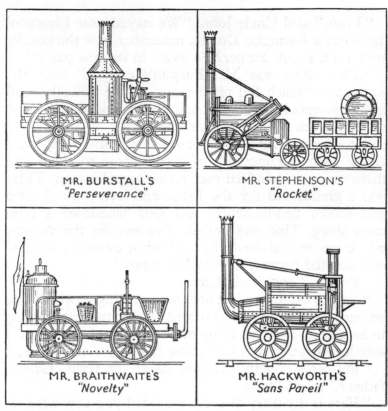

MR. BURSTALL'S
"Perseverance"

MR. STEPHENSON'S
"Rocket"

MR. BRAITHWAITE'S
"Novelty"

MR. HACKWORTH'S
"Sans Pareil"

(You will find more about the very early steam engines on page 42.)

"The trials were held on a piece of finished track at Rainhill, nine miles from Liverpool, in October 1829 and I was one of the judges. There were three of us, Nicholas Wood of Killingworth, John Rastrick of Stourbridge and myself. The other two knew more about steam engines, but as I was one of the Directors of the railway line, I knew the kind of engine we wanted. I took you along too, didn't I, John? Can you remember it?"

21

"I can," said Uncle John. "We stayed near Liverpool for about a fortnight. Do you remember how the ROCKET arrived on a cart, Father? So smart in its new paint."

"Then there was Mr. Burstall's engine," said Mr. Kennedy, "which fell off the cart on the turnpike road from Liverpool to Rainhill and was damaged. He spent the first week of the trials mending it."

"It was exciting, James, just like a horse race," said Uncle John. "Thousands of people came to watch and there were two hundred men acting as policemen. There was a grandstand for the ladies and everyone cheered and waved handkerchiefs and hats whenever a train came along. That was not often except for the ROCKET, which ran up and down the track while everyone shouted and laughed because it looked so funny."

"Funny!" exclaimed James.

"Yes, to us, for we had not seen anything moving alone without a horse. I heard someone say, 'It makes me giddy to look at it. It seems to fly on the wings of the wind.' I wonder what they would say now to our present speeds."

"But what exactly did you do at the trials, Grandfather?" asked James.

"Here is my diary of 1829. I can tell you now what we did each day."

Monday, 6th October. Met Mr. Wood and Mr. Rastrick at the Railway Office in Liverpool. Mr. Booth, Treasurer of the Railway, gave us the rules of the competition, which we discussed.

"You must remember, James, that nothing like this had ever been done before, so we had to find a way of testing these engines. Later we went to Rainhill and looked at the track and the engines."

Tuesday, 7th October. Went to Rainhill to talk over again what task we would make them do.

"So that was two days you wasted in talking," said Mrs. Kennedy.

"Perhaps so," replied Mr. Kennedy; "but there was no need for us to hurry. We watched Mr. Brandreth exercising his horses but we did not take his machine seriously. The ROCKET, of course, was running up and down to everyone's amusement but that was the only one ready. Mr. Burstall was mending his and neither of the other two was finished. It was great fun watching the engineers and their workmen trying to get the machines to work; but that evening we went back to Liverpool and talked over our plans and settled the task that we wanted each engine to do. This we had printed for the competitors."

"And what was the task, Grandfather?" asked James.

"We decided that the engines must not only go fast but also keep on running, for the distance from Liverpool to Manchester was thirty miles. We did not want the engine we chose to break down on the way. So we set up two posts over a mile apart and the engines had to go to and fro ten times. We would note the time they took and how often they stopped. We also decided to weigh the engines, to weigh the amount of fuel they used and how much water they took. You see, James, all these things would affect the cost of running our railway."

Wednesday, 8th October. An exciting day, for Braithwaite burst his bellows and Hackworth's boiler began to break and all the time the ROCKET was running up and down to everyone's cheering.

23

Thursday, 9th October. We settled down to testing. Mr. Rastrick went to post 1 and Mr. Wood to post 2 with note-books and second watches which they had set together. They noted down the times as the engines ran past the posts and other details.

After the ROCKET had finished the test satisfactorily, we found that the NOVELTY would not be ready until Monday and that Mr. Hackworth still needed more time, so we postponed any more trials until Monday of the second week.

Friday, 10th October. Mr. Braithwaite came to Liverpool to see us and asked to be allowed to run his test on Saturday. We tried to persuade him that the joints of the boiler would set better if left over the week-end but he would not be persuaded.

Saturday, 11th October. We tested the NOVELTY which had no tender like the others. Suddenly while it was running its trial, the feed to the boiler burst and water was flying about in all directions. That brought the trial to an end for that day.

Tuesday, 14th October. When we went along at eight o'clock in the morning, we found that Mr. Hackworth had been running his engine all night, as he was anxious to get it right, and this meant that the water in the boiler was still hot. Another test was to find out how long it took the different engines to get up steam, for that was another important point for the railway. To save time, we decided to let the SANS PAREIL run its test that morning and find out how long it took to get up steam later. Unfortunately on its 8th trip by the grandstand, after it had run about 27 miles, the pump went wrong and a lead plug melted in the fire tube. It was too late to start again when the repairs were completed as it was getting dark.

24

Wednesday, 15th October. We found that Mr. Braithwaite had his boiler in pieces and the workmen still on it. It was late by the time they had fitted it together and started the test. On the second trip the joints of the boiler gave way and it was decided to withdraw the engine as unsatisfactory.

Mr. Hackworth all this time was very annoyed with everything and now formally asked by letter for retrial saying that his engine was better than it had seemed at the trials. However, we thought of the huge amount of fuel used and decided not to let it run again. Then Hackworth said the weighing machine was wrong but still we did not allow a retrial.

Mr. Burstall brought out his engine and ran it up and down but it was obviously of no use so he said that he would not enter it for the competition. Thus there was nothing else to do but declare that Mr. Stephenson's ROCKET was the best engine and he won the prize.

"Yes," said Uncle John, "the ROCKET was the one. It was the only engine to keep going all the time and to do all the tests, so the judges agreed that it was the best. Why! it travelled at 29 miles an hour and that was unheard of in those days."

"Well, at last the railway was finished in the summer of 1830," continued Mr. Kennedy, "and we were all awaiting the opening day. I don't think that you can imagine, James, how excited everyone was. Nothing like this had ever been seen before. Perhaps if I read some parts from this letter you will know a little how a steam engine appeared to us. Remember that we had known only horse-drawn coaches up to that time! This letter is written by a young lady, Miss Fanny Kemble, a friend of Mr. Stephenson's who had a trip on the railway a few weeks before it was opened."

We were introduced to the little engine which was to drag us along the rails. She (for they make these curious little fire-horses all mares) consisted of a boiler, a stove, a platform, a bench, and behind the bench a barrel containing enough water to prevent her being thirsty for fifteen miles. She goes upon two wheels, which are her feet and are moved by bright steel legs called pistons; these are moved by steam and as more steam is given so they move the wheels faster; and when it is wished to lessen the speed, the steam, which unless allowed to escape, would burst the boiler, rushes through a safety valve, into the air. The reins, bridle and bit of this wonderful animal is a small steel handle, which gives the steam to the pistons and which a child could manage. The coals which are its oats, were under the bench, and there was a small glass tube fixed to the boiler with water in it which shows by its fullness or emptiness, when the animal wants water. There is a chimney to the stove, but as they burn coke there is none of the dreadful black smoke which accompanies the progress of a steamship.

This snorting little animal, which I felt inclined to pat, was harnessed to our carriage, and Mr. Stephenson having taken me on the bench with him, we started at about ten miles an hour. The steam horse being unable to go up and down hill, the road was kept at a certain level, and appeared sometimes to sink below the surface of the earth and sometimes to rise above it. Almost at starting, it was cut through the solid rock which formed a wall on either side of it, about sixty feet high. (Olive Mount Cutting.)

You cannot imagine how strange it seemed to be travelling between these rocky walls, which are already clothed with moss, and ferns and grasses; and when I thought that these great masses of stone had been cut to allow our travelling so far below the surface of the earth I felt no fairy tale was half so wonderful as what I saw.

We had come now fifteen miles, and stopped where the road

26

crosses a wide and deep valley. Mr. Stephenson made me alight and led me down to the bottom of this valley, over which in order to keep his road level, he had thrown a viaduct of nine arches, one of which is 70 feet high, through which we saw the whole of this beautiful valley. (Sankey Viaduct.)

The engine having received its supply of water, the carriage was placed behind it, for it cannot turn, and was set off at its upmost speed, 35 miles an hour; swifter than a bird flies (for they tried the experiment with a snipe). When I closed my eyes, this feeling of flying was delightful and strange beyond description; yet strange as it was, I had not the slightest fear.

Now a word or two about the master of all these marvels. He is a man from 50 to 55 years of age; his face is fine, though careworn, and bears an expression of deep thoughtfulness.

It has taken four years to bring this great undertaking to an end. The railway will be opened upon the 15th of next month. The Duke of Wellington is coming down to be present on the occasion, and I suppose, that, with the thousands of spectators, there will never have been such an exciting scene. The whole cost of the work (including the engines and the carriages) will have been £830,000 and it is already worth double that sum. The Directors have kindly offered us three places for the opening, which is a great favour, for people are willing to pay almost anything for a seat, I understand.

"September 15th arrived," continued Mr. Kennedy, "the day on which our railway was to be declared open by the Duke of Wellington. At that time he was Prime Minister.

"The weather was dull and before the ride was over it was raining heavily but everyone said that it was a wonderful sight. We had planned, James, to have a procession of our steam engines and carriages from Liverpool to Manchester and back again so that everyone could see the line was really working. The trains carried about 800 visitors with a band and flags and a special carriage for the Duke and his party. Here is a picture of it.

The Duke of Wellington's special carriage

"It was said to be like a Greek chariot, painted to look like gold, with crimson cloth drapery and the Duke's coronet on top. As we travelled along, people gathered by the track cheering and shouting and waving their hats and handkerchiefs. It was an exciting ride!"

"I did not enjoy it," said old Mrs. Kennedy. "I did not like travelling so fast and I sat waiting for the time when I could get down on to the firm ground once more."

"Oh Mother, you are old-fashioned," laughed Uncle John.

"Perhaps I am, but I still do not like the things. I still like to travel in my own carriage."

"There are not many who think as you do, Mary," said Mr. Kennedy. "For those who cannot afford to keep a carriage, the railway is a great deal better than the stage coach. Many had walked miles to see us go by on that opening day. But I will read another letter to you, James, which describes the happenings. Here it is!—

Liverpool was never so full of strangers, all the inns in the town were crowded to overflowing and carriages stood in the streets all night, for want of room in stable yards.

On the morning of Wednesday, the people of the town and of the country began very early to gather near the railway. The weather was fine but dull. From before nine o'clock until ten the entrance of the station was crowded by splendid carriages from which people were alighting to seek their places as shown on their tickets. There were eight engines drawing thirty-three carriages filled with elegantly dressed persons. Each train had silken flags of different colours flying above the carriages. There were three bands playing, one of them in a carriage of one train.

The firing of a gun and the cheers of the crowd announced the arrival of the Duke of Wellington and his friends. The bands played "See the Conquering Hero Comes" and his railway carriage was attached to the Northumbrian locomotive engine. I was in the first train after the grand cars, and was drawn by the PHOENIX. My train consisted of three open and two closed carriages. There were thousands of spectators who were kept out of the way by soldiers and railway police. A few minutes before eleven all was ready for the journey. The signal gun being fired, we started.

Our first thoughts, from the road being so level, were that it must be monotonous and uninteresting. It is the contrary; for, as the road does not rise and fall like the ground over which we pass, but goes nearly at a level, whether the land be high or low, we are at the moment drawn through a hill and find ourselves 70 feet below the surface and at another we are as many feet above the green fields, looking down upon the roofs of farm houses and see the distant hills and woods.

Our speed gradually increased till, entering the Olive Mount Cutting, we rushed through at 24 miles an hour. By this time, the Duke was far ahead of us; we saw them gliding beautifully over the Sankey Viaduct. The fields below us were filled with thousands of people who cheered as we passed; carriages filled the narrow lanes. Soon we reached Parkside, 17 miles from Liverpool, in about four minutes under the hour. Here the engines were to receive fresh water and most of us alighted and were walking about, talking of the journey. Then a crowd gathered and there was a delay and we soon heard the reason for it. Mr. Huskisson, after shaking hands with the Duke of Wellington, fell under an approaching engine, injuring his leg. The poor gentleman was put in a carriage with his wife, a doctor and Mr. Stephenson, and set off towards Manchester.

We stayed another hour, uncertain what to do, the Duke surrounded by the Directors and a mournful group of gentlemen. At first, it was thought best to return to Liverpool; but then the Borough Reeve of Manchester said that, if the procession did not reach Manchester, where a great multitude of people was assembled, he should be fearful for the peace of the town. The Duke said the whole party should go on. On reaching the twentieth mile post we had a beautiful view of Rivington Pike, and Blackstone Edge, and at the twenty-first the smoke of Manchester appeared.

Groups of people continued to cheer us, but we could not reply, and from the twenty-fourth mile post we found ourselves with spectators on either side all the way to Manchester. Upon one bridge the motto "Vote by Ballot" was seen; in a field near Eccles, a poor and wretchedly dressed man had his loom close to the roadside and was weaving with all his might; cries of "No *Corn Laws*" were occasionally heard, and for about two miles the cheerings of the crowd were mingled with the hissing and hooting from a few.

We reached the warehouses about three o'clock and stopped. In the upper rooms a most elegant cold meal had been prepared for a thousand people. At half past four we moved away to Liverpool, where we arrived about seven o'clock.

So ended a pageant which is said to have been greater than anything seen before. We spoke with many gentlemen, used to public meetings, and they thought that not fewer than 500,000 people must have seen the procession.

"Well, there you are, my lad," said Mr. Kennedy. "The railway was finished. The next day it started to carry passengers with goods. About 140 people went on the first trip. So it has continued ever since."

A Great Success

"And was the railway a success, Grandfather?" asked James.

"Oh yes, even better than we had hoped. We had expected to carry about four hundred passengers a day. We were wrong. Soon there were over a thousand a day and we had to order more trucks and locomotives to carry the goods, for all we had planned were needed to carry the people. Of course, we made more and more money, so everyone who had lent money began to get money back on their shares. The railway proved that a public line would pay if it was built between two busy towns like Liverpool and Manchester."

"Lots of people came here for a holiday, James," said Uncle John, "so that they could travel on the railway and tell their friends about it."

"Other people came to inspect our line, just as we had

gone to Stockton," said Mr. Kennedy, "for when our line proved to be a success, there were plans for many other lines. When these people were trying to get their Bills through Parliament, they talked about the success of our line to prove how useful theirs would be.

"So you see, James, the railway building is just beginning. By the time you are grown up there will be thousands of miles of line going in all directions across the country. It makes one proud to have had a hand in the beginning of this great adventure."

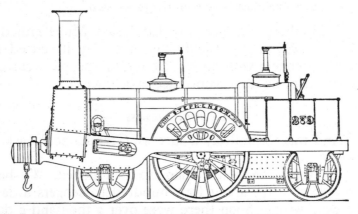

This is a locomotive of the Crewe type which was in use on the Liverpool and Manchester Railway in 1845. Notice how different it is from the earlier engines, although it was built only 15 years later. Already this locomotive is not unlike some of the small shunting engines you see to-day.

Although the two lines were not joined until 1845, the Liverpool and Manchester Railway and the Grand Junction Railway had always been closely connected, with several directors on both boards. From 1843, there was one locomotive department at Crewe, and this engine was one of the first to be designed and built there.

"Don't think that you will not see any excitements in the early days of the railways, my lad," said Uncle John. "There is this dispute now about the *gauges*."

"What is that?"

"Do you know what the gauge is?"

"Oh, yes, the distance apart of the wheels and so of the lines on which the trains run."

"Right! Now remember that Mr. Stephenson had to make his first engines with the same gauge as was used at Killingworth Colliery for the coal trucks, that is four feet eight and a half inches. He made his experiments, you see, on the coal lines, and as the engine worked he did not think to alter the distance of the wheels and rails later on. So all his railways were built with the same gauge. Other engineers, however, think that a wider gauge would give faster and safer trains. Mr. Brunel, the chief engineer of the Great Western Railway, is one of them and his company use a broad gauge, with the lines seven feet apart. Then, in East Anglia, the Eastern Counties Railway uses a five foot gauge. While each railway is separate from the other, the different gauges don't matter. But you can see the difficulty when two different gauges come to the same town."

"Yes, the engines and carriages cannot run on the lines of the other company."

"Last year the Great Western laid a line to Gloucester where the Midland Railway already had a line. Everyone saw the difficulty of two gauges in the same station. All the people who wanted to travel beyond Gloucester on the other line had to get out with their luggage and move into another train; the goods had to be unpacked from one truck, carried to another and loaded in. It is a great waste of time. It is clear there must be one gauge only in the country, for as more railways are built, what is happening at Gloucester to-day will happen over and over again. The problem is, which gauge?"

"What a problem!" said James. "Whoever loses will have to relay their lines, and that costs money."

"That's right. It is also an argument between the two best engineers in the country about which gauge is the better. Mr. Stephenson and Mr. Brunel are against one another, and they cannot agree. So Parliament has set up a Royal Commission to take reports from the engineers, to make experiments, to visit Gloucester and see if the change from one train to another is really the waste of time some people claim it to be."

"What will happen then, Uncle?"

"There will be a Report published and from that Parliament will probably pass an Act forcing one gauge on the whole country."

(You can see what the Commission advised on page 57.)

Trains running on narrow and broad gauge lines

HERE YOU WILL FIND MORE ABOUT THE RAILWAYS IN THE FIRST PART OF THE NINETEENTH CENTURY

The People in the Story

First, how do we know all this? You may have been saying to yourself as you read about John Kennedy: 'Oh, this is only a story!' Yes, it is a story, but it happens to be a true one. All those things you have been reading about really happened. It is one of the stories which make up history.

Then you say, how do we know about it when it all happened more than one hundred years ago?

JOHN KENNEDY, you will remember, was a cotton manufacturer and a very successful one. He went to the meeting in Liverpool in 1824. He was one of a party who visited the Stockton and Darlington Railway in 1825. He was one of the judges at the Rainhill Trials. All these events you can find described in the records of the Liverpool and Manchester Railway. At the Science Museum in London you will see his name printed with others on various papers.

John Kennedy with other important men of Manchester was a member of the Literary and Philosophical Society.

This Society was interested in all current affairs and John Kennedy read several papers to the members during the first years of the nineteenth century. Later these were printed as one book and John Kennedy wrote a short account of his early life as an introduction.

John Kennedy

Some other details of his life we can learn from a book published by the sons

35

of James M'Connel, John Kennedy's partner and grand-father of young James in the story. This book, published in 1861, sets out to prove that the family are entitled to a coat of arms, and amongst other things there is quite a lot about John Kennedy. There is therefore evidence in books about these people.

GEORGE STEPHENSON was born at Wylam, eight miles west of Newcastle-on-Tyne, in 1781. His parents were so poor that they could afford only one room in a cottage. One of his earliest tasks was to keep his younger brothers and sisters out of the way of the coal wagons which were dragged by horses along the wooden tramway in front of the cottage door.

George Stephenson

After various jobs at collieries learning all he could about Newcomen's pumping engine, he became engine-wright at Killingworth Colliery in 1812. Among other things like cobbling shoes and dressmaking (to earn extra money), Stephenson learned to write, to read and do arithmetic. He learnt all in the evenings when he had finished his long day's work at the pit. He studied his engine carefully and gradually made improvements on it. His employers allowed him to alter the engine and even gave him money to build a new one and allowed other workmen at the colliery to help him. So he gradually learnt the way steam could work and he built his engines aided by his son Robert. (You will find other details about his life in other notes of this section.)

There is no space in this book to tell you about the lives of all the engineers and inventors you will read about in the next pages. If you wish to know more about any of them, get a book from your local library.

Railways before the Steam Engine was Invented

Long before the invention of the steam engine, goods had been carried in trucks with wheels that ran on parallel rails. In the Middle Ages, goods were carried in baskets on the backs of horses. Stone, slate, and coal were very heavy goods for horses to carry in this way, and in Germany a simple railway was in use in the early part of the sixteenth century. The trucks were pushed by men, for already they had found that the wheels moved more easily on rails than on the rough roads of those days. We know this from a book which was published in 1556 with pictures and diagrams of how they worked. Here you can see a miner pushing a wagon of ore out of a mine.

In England rails were first laid in the Newcastle district, and at the beginning of the eighteenth century there were also short lines in North Wales to carry slate, near Bath for stone and in South Wales for coal and iron. It was the coal trade in the Newcastle district which led to the laying down of miles of rails. There were always boats arriving to fetch the coal and you can see how much more coal could be moved by one horse in this way than by pannier baskets.

There is a picture of a Newcastle truck or chaldron in 1764 on page 12. The wagons were drawn by horses along the rails to the river where the ships tied up against wooden structures called *staithes*. As you can see in the next picture, the wagons were tipped at the end of the

staithe by a pulley and the coal fell into the boat below. In 1720 there were more than 20,000 horses pulling trucks in this way around Newcastle and the number was always increasing. You will see that it needed one man and one horse for every wagon-load of coal. The track was usually so rough that the man was needed to clear the way and act as a brake when the wagon went downhill.

More boats, however, came to the staithes for coal and so mines were opened up further from the staithes and the railway lines became longer. Sometimes it was not possible for the colliery owner to lay the track across his own land, so he asked permission to do so from another landowner, promising to pay a certain sum of money. If the owner of the land refused, the colliery owner asked Parliament to pass an Act forcing the landowner to have the railway lines over his land. The first Act of this kind was passed in 1758 for a line near Leeds.

It was not until 1801 that an Act was passed by Parliament permitting the building of a railway line which anyone could use. It was called the Grand Surrey Iron Railway and ran for $9\frac{1}{2}$ miles from Croydon to the River Thames at Wandsworth. Unlike the railways of to-day, any goods carrier who had wagons which would run on the rails and the horses to pull them could use the track by paying a certain sum of money. The track was a *plateway* and this made it easier for the goods carriers to use the wagons on the roads, as you can see on page 12.

By 1820, it was clear that the railways were better than the roads for carrying heavy goods and that iron rails were better than wooden ones, but the engineers could not agree about the best way of pulling the trucks.

Here are the ways from which they had to choose:

1. By horses;
2. By stationary engines pulling the trucks on ropes;
3. By locomotives driven by steam.

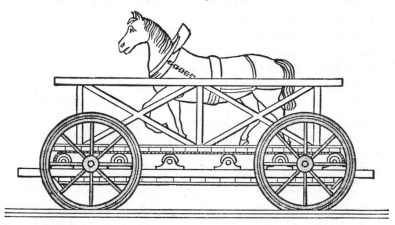

This strange machine was built by Mr. Brandreth in 1829 (see page 23). As the horse's feet went to and fro, they moved the wheels underneath.

Have you read a story about a young man, James Watt, who watched the steam lifting the lid from a kettle? Did the story then tell you that he invented a new steam engine after he had seen the power of the steam coming from the kettle?

Of course he was not the first to notice the power of steam. For hundreds of years before Watt was born, men had been trying to find a way of using heat to drive their machines. There was also an idea that steam might drive a carriage along the road—a Frenchman in the seventeenth century was shut away as mad because he believed this.

Another Frenchman, Denis Papin, in 1681, boiled bones in an enclosed vessel under pressure and to prevent the vessel from blowing up he invented a *safety valve*. He thought that the jelly from the bones, flavoured with sugar and lemon juice, was very good for him. He would be surprised that he is remembered for his safety valve, which is still used to-day, and not for his cooking! Have you examined the safety valve on a pressure cooker?

Thomas Savery built the first steam engine to do useful work in 1698. It was very simple, for steam pushed directly on the water, but it was very wasteful of fuel since, as soon as the vessel had been heated, it was cooled by cold water to *condense* the steam, only to be heated again by fresh steam. As the steam was difficult to control, it could not lift the water very far. We remember Savery, however, because he was the first man to use the word *horsepower* to measure the amount of work done by a machine.

Then came Thomas Newcomen, a blacksmith at Dartmouth in Devon. He invented the steam engine that George Stephenson studied.

Newcomen's engine was very clumsy, creaking and banging as it pumped water from coal and tin mines. Can you see why it wasted coal? For every movement of the *beam*, fresh steam had to fill the *cylinder*.

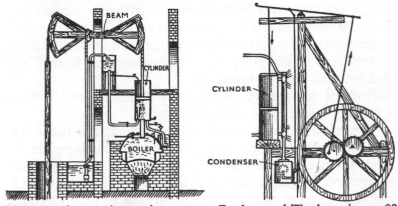

Newcomen's pumping engine, 1712   Boulton and Watt's engine, 1788

Watt noticed this waste in 1769 when he was repairing one of these engines. He decided that the cylinder must be kept hot and yet the steam must be condensed to make the *vacuum*—to condense the steam without cooling the cylinder. Thus he added a condenser which could be kept cold and wrapped up the cylinder to keep it hot. You can see this in the diagram. Watt also invented other improvements. (If you wish to know more about these, get a book on Watt or engines from your library.) We honour Watt in the word 'kilowatt,' that is, a thousand watts, another way of measuring power.

All these engines were stationary. Some, however, pulled trucks on rails with ropes. They were used in the mining districts, usually hauling trucks up steep slopes.

Moving Steam Engines (*Locomotives*)

You will remember that men had thought of having moving steam engines in the seventeenth century. In 1769, another Frenchman called Cugnot built a carriage moved by steam to pull guns, but when it crashed into a wall, it was shut away by the Government as too dangerous. Later, William Murdoch, who worked for Watt fixing his engines into the mines in Cornwall, made a moving engine in 1786, but he did not get any encouragement from Watt and his idea was not taken up.

Perhaps you are wondering why it was so long before a moving steam engine was invented?

You must remember that the steam engines made by Watt were very heavy so they would need much power to move themselves and a load. Then, too, the roads were so rough and in places so steep that it needed a powerful machine to move along them. Finally, there were no tools for making the exact parts needed.

The first moving steam engines were used on rails and not on the rough roads.

Improving the Steam Engine

Do you know the principal parts of a steam locomotive?

1. The *firebox* and boiler where the energy of the fuel is changed into steam.
2. The cylinders where the energy of the steam moves the *pistons* which in turn move the wheels.
3. The chassis or framework, the wheels, and *axles* which use the energy and by means of the *drawbar* pull the rest of the train.

What were the problems to solve in order to build an engine which would move more quickly while pulling a heavy load?

1. To get enough draught to keep up a hot fire.
2. To have a large heating surface in a small space.

On these next pages, you will see how some of the early inventors tried to solve these problems.

Richard Trevithick built an engine in 1804 which ran on a tramway at Merthyr Tydvil in South Wales. It was so heavy that it often crushed the cast-iron rails. He built CATCH ME WHO CAN in 1808 to run on a circular track in North London. A high fence was set up around the track and people paid to go in and see the engine. Here it is:

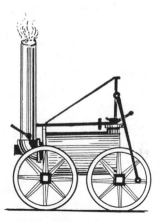

But Trevithick was not a business man and no one was very interested, except a colliery owner at Wylam near Newcastle who ordered an engine; but it was not of any use. It was near Wylam that Stephenson was born and, although he had moved some miles away, he probably heard of this experiment.

43

Do you remember how the bad roads were hindering industry at the beginning of the nineteenth century? By moving trucks on rails, the colliery owners had overcome the bad roads. But more ships were arriving at the staithes for coal and the horses could pull only one or two wagons at a time.

During the Napoleonic Wars fodder was difficult to get and, as there were over 20,000 horses around Newcastle alone, the colliery owners were forced to look for a cheaper and quicker way of moving the coal to the ships.

In 1811, Murray and Blenkinsop of Leeds, using Trevithick's design, built a *cog engine*. This was the first locomotive to work successfully, for it drew 27 wagons at a time, but its speed was only 3 miles an hour!

Puffing Billy

PUFFING BILLY was built in 1813 by William Hedley, an engineer at Wylam Colliery. He used a colliery pumping engine as a model, the vertical cylinders causing the beams to rise and fall which turned the wheels through *gearing*. Can you guess how it got its name? Both these engines ran on smooth rails.

LOCOMOTION NO. I was built by George Stephenson in 1825 for the Stockton and Darlington Railway and he drove it on the opening day. You will see that the wheels are *coupled* together and that it works like Puffing Billy.

ROYAL GEORGE was built by Timothy Hackworth, the engineer for the Stockton and Darlington Railway.

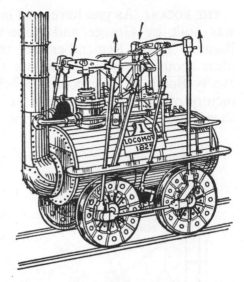

It had a much larger heating surface in the boiler than any engine yet made, and it was the first locomotive to have a direct drive. (The piston moves the wheel directly without any gearing in between.)

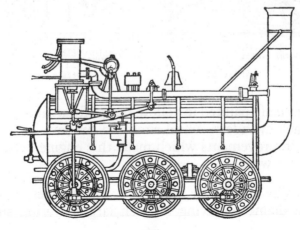

THE ROCKET. As you have read in the story, this engine was built by George and Robert Stephenson for the Rainhill Trials. Remember that they took all the latest ideas about locomotives and put them into this engine. Henry Booth of Liverpool also helped them. There is a picture of the engine on page 21. Here is a diagram to show the main parts of the engine, and its size.

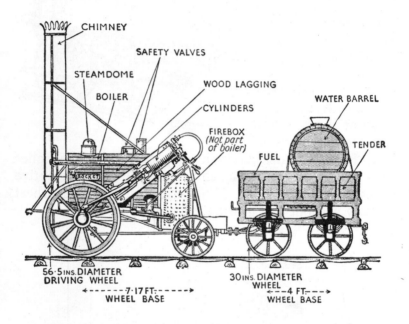

It was gaily painted in yellow except for a white chimney and black cylinders, wheel rims and firebox.

The improvements which made this engine better than the others were:

1. Inside the boiler were 25 copper tubes, 3 inches in diameter, giving a much larger heating surface.

46

We call this a multi-tubular boiler (thus solving the second problem set out on page 43).

2. Direct drive by connecting rod and *crank*.
3. Better valves which controlled more accurately the amount of steam entering the cylinders.

At Rainhill, Stephenson found that the steeply inclined cylinders made the Rocket unsteady when it was going at speed. It wobbled so much that, even if he could make it go faster, he knew that it would be dangerous. So he put the cylinders in a more horizontal position, as you can see in the Rocket itself if you visit the Science Museum in London where you can see this famous locomotive.

Here are pictures of Stephenson's next locomotives:

THE NORTHUMBRIAN led the procession at the opening in 1830 of the Liverpool and Manchester Railway (page 28). Notice the nearly horizontal cylinders and central *buffer* of padded leather at the back of the tender, which was better than the earlier ones. This engine also had a firebox as part of the boiler and it also had the first *smokebox*.

THE PLANET was a great improvement, the cylinders being inside at the bottom of the smokebox, with the *driving wheels* at the rear.

Tremendous improvements have been made on locomotives from that day until this. Here are some of the problems which faced the engineers after 1830:

1. To make the engine go faster and pull heavier trains the engineers wanted the locomotive to have more power. To gain this, they made the boiler longer.

1829 The Rocket   length of boiler 6 ft.
1832 The Bury   ,,   ,,   ,,   8 ft.
1845 The Long-boiler ,,   ,,   ,,   12 ft.

The speed of normal passenger trains increased from an average of 15 m.p.h. in 1830 to an average of 37 m.p.h. in 1845.

2. As the speed became greater and the engine longer, the locomotive was found to rock from side to side when running full out. A pair of *trailing wheels* was put at the back. They were called 'trailing' because they had no connection with the coupled driving wheels.

3. The crank-axles of the 6-wheeled locomotives often broke when running round bends on the track and the cylinders were put outside. After 1833, when the boiler became longer, the front part was placed on a bogie, a small truck with four or six wheels. These wheels do not form part of the driving system and the boiler rests by a swivel-pin or plate which allows the bogie to turn on its own. As it is free, it reduces the strain and jolting going round curves and lessens the danger of the train leaving the rails, which might happen if a long, rigid wheel-base turned.

4. At first the locomotives made clouds of smoke, until the Government said they must burn coke; but later improvements needed coal. In 1841 Samuel Hall designed a system of air tubes to prevent smoking and also the Brick Arch which, by making the hot gases take a roundabout route, heated all the firebox.

5. Coupled driving wheels gave a better grip on the rails when a heavy train was starting.

6. The development of signalling was necessary before speed could be increased with safety. (See page 69.)

7. Better brakes were also needed before trains could travel at speed with safety and in 1870 George Westinghouse invented the automatic pressure brake.

8. The stream-line shape of modern locomotives offers less resistance to the wind and throws the smoke clear of the driver's vision.

You cannot expect a truck with smooth wheels to balance on smooth rails and then to be drawn along without falling off. There must be something on either the rail or the wheel to prevent this. This something is called a *flange*. You can either have a smooth rail and a flange on the wheel or a smooth wheel and the flange on the rail. Here they are in these diagrams.

Flange on the wheels

Flange on the rails

You remember (page 37) that the earliest railways were used in Germany. These trucks ran on smooth WOODEN rails and were kept on by the wheels. The earliest truck, which still exists in a Berlin Museum, has flanged wooden wheels like this with metal axles.

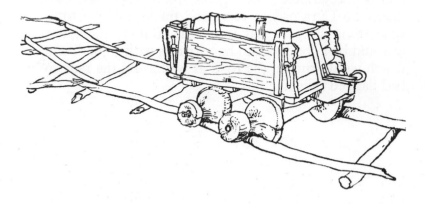

During the eighteenth century, there were some improvements to the track. Oak *sleepers* were laid across the track first and the rails were nailed to them. Then it was found that the rails wore out very quickly on bends or slopes, so pieces of iron were laid along them in these places. Finally, in 1767, *cast iron* rails were used at the iron works at Coalbrookdale in Shropshire. It was here that Abraham Darby was experimenting in smelting iron ore with coke, and the story goes that at one time he had more iron smelted than anyone wanted to buy. So he laid it down as rails. He meant to take it up when he had a customer, but it wore so well that he persuaded others to try iron rails too! They were used in the Newcastle district where the mine owners found that a horse could pull two trucks on the flat on iron rails.

The next change was the coming of the plateway. John Curr was the manager of the Duke of Norfolk's colliery near Sheffield, and in 1776 decided to lay a railway to carry coal into the town. The men who had carted the coal or owned pack-horses thought they would lose their jobs, so they rioted, took up the wooden rails and burned them. So Curr had to relay the track and this time he used stone sleepers and iron rails. But he thought that it would be a good idea to have trucks with smooth wheels which would run on the road as well as on the rails so he laid flanged rails like this:

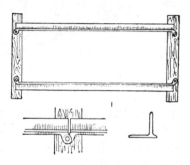

The cast iron rails had a flange on the inner side about 3 inches high and the trucks were horse drawn. This was known as a plateway and became very popular in South Wales. It was also used on the Grand Surrey Iron Railway (page 39) which had rails like this:

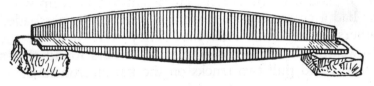

Here are pictures of other experiments to find the perfect rail.

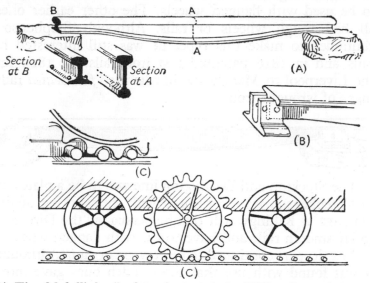

Section at B

Section at A

(A)

(B)

(C)

(C)

(A) The *fish-bellied rails* of cast iron made by William Jessop in 1789.
(B) The *chair* invented by Thomas Barnes to hold the rail to the sleeper.
(C) Cog-wheel used on the rack railway at Leeds.

The engineers who were trying to build a steam engine were still sure that smooth rails and wheels, even with the flange on one or other, would not 'bite' but would whirl round and round, so Trevithick gave his driving wheels rough surfaces, Murray used the *rack rail*, and at Wylam Blackett had a man scattering ashes on the rails before the engine came along!

Stephenson carried out many tests with loaded trucks and found that they would 'bite' even when moving at speed. He was also interested in the *wrought iron* rails which had been made in Scotland.

Stephenson's first engine, called the BLUCHER, which ran at Killingworth in 1814, was the first locomotive to be used with flanged wheels. The other earlier ones all had rough wheels or rails. Although Stephenson continued to make this type, he was still interested in rails and in 1816 patented cast iron rails. In 1829 for the Liverpool to Manchester line he used *fish-bellied* rails made of wrought iron.

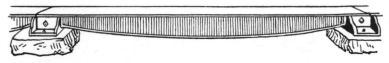

The Stockton and Darlington line was to be a plateway but Stephenson was so pleased with the working of the BLUCHER at Killingworth that he persuaded the Directors to lay smooth rails and have trucks with flanged wheels.

The sleepers continued to be of wood or stone, although it was found with use that the wooden ones gave more comfortable travelling and gradually the stone ones were replaced. They were not always laid across the track. Sometimes at terminal stations or on bridges they were laid along the rail; but this was not the usual practice as it was more difficult to remove them if they were in this position.

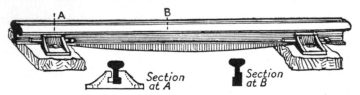

The *bull-head* (the upper part was wider than the lower) developed easily from Stephenson's rail, as you will see if you compare the diagrams. The rail fitted as before, into chairs or steel holders which were spiked to the sleeper. To hold the rail really firm, wooden wedges

54

were placed between the outside of the chair and the rail. To-day, however, there are flat-bottomed rails held to the sleepers by clips, as you can see in the next diagram.

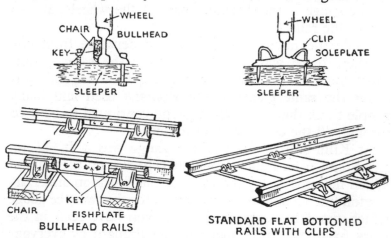

BULLHEAD RAILS

STANDARD FLAT BOTTOMED RAILS WITH CLIPS

The arrangement of the wheels of a modern locomotive is interesting because locomotives can be classed according to the arrangement and number of the bogie, coupled and trailing wheels which it possesses. For example, here are some famous types of locomotives:

The AMERICAN type or 4—4—0 which has a leading four-wheeled bogie and four coupled wheels, and no trailing wheels.

The ATLANTIC type or 4—4—2 which has a leading four-wheeled bogie, four coupled wheels and a single pair of trailing wheels beneath the firebox.

The PACIFIC type or 4—6—2 which has a leading four-wheeled bogie, six coupled wheels and a single pair of trailing wheels.

4-4-2 ATLANTIC

4-4-0 AMERICAN

4-6-2 PACIFIC

Gauge

The gauge is the distance apart of the wheels, and so also of the rails.

While the railway lines remained separate from one another, there was no need to have the same gauge. Most tracks in Britain were about 4 ft. 6 in. This was about the same gauge as the Romans used and many people think that the Roman gauge continued to be used through all the centuries that followed.

At Killingworth Colliery the gauge was 4 ft. 8½ in. and Stephenson built the BLUCHER to run on these lines. When he came to lay the track of the Stockton and Darlington line he used the same gauge, for that was the gauge which fitted his engines. But, as you have read in the story (page 33), this gauge was not thought by everyone to be the best.

The Royal Commission on Gauges, 1845, sat to consider the evidence put forward by Brunel for a broader gauge than the one used by Stephenson. The broad gauge party said that the movement of goods and people from one train to another at Gloucester caused little delay but the narrow gauge party did all they could to make the confusion at Gloucester as bad as possible. They realized that, in future, when there were more towns in which the two different gauges met, there would be a great loss of time, taking the country as a whole, and they were out to win the battle of the gauges for all time. When the Commission visited Gloucester to see the movement for themselves they were horrified by the clamour, which the narrow gauge party had arranged. The porters were shouting out the names and addresses on the parcels as loudly as they could. They were throwing them down to other porters on the platforms who threw them noisily into other trucks. Some were getting lost and then everyone raced about looking for them. Some of the trucks were suddenly found to contain the wrong parcels and had to be unloaded hurriedly. All the time the poor passengers were trying to make their way from one train to another with their luggage, getting in the way of the porters, which in its turn led to more argument and yelling. (I think the porters enjoyed themselves that day, don't you? But what about the passengers?)

The Commission decided that there must be only one gauge in the country and chose the narrow one, so in 1846 the Gauge Act was passed by Parliament, stating that any future railway line must be laid with a gauge of 4 ft. 8½ in. but that the Great Western Railway could continue to use the gauge of 7 ft. 0¼ in. Gradually this company laid a third rail on all its tracks so that it could use locomotives of either gauge on every line.

Parkside Station in 1831. You can read about this picture on the next page.

How Engines got Fresh Supplies of Water

Do you remember how on the opening day when Mr. Huskisson, the Member of Parliament for Liverpool, was killed, the trains had stopped at Parkside? Do you remember why?

At first the engines could carry water for only 15 miles. Look at the picture of Parkside Station in 1831. Notice that there are no raised platforms as we have to-day. You can also see the *water-crane* which was used then. It is not very different from those you see at stations to-day.

Have you travelled on a train which ran for three or four hours without a stop? How does this engine get fresh supplies of water? You probably know that it scoops it up as it goes along. This *water-scoop tender*, as it is called, was invented in 1860 by John Ramsbottom. He was a famous engineer after Stephenson, who for a long time was in charge of the great railway workshops at Crewe. Here is a diagram of a water-scoop tender.

This is a picture of the first passenger railway coach ever built. Stephenson ordered it for the Stockton and Darlington Railway in 1825. It was drawn by a horse along the rails and held six passengers inside and fifteen outside. So, you see, not only does it look very like a road coach but passengers were also carried in the same way as they had been on the road. Would you like to sit on the top of a railway coach to-day? Remember that this coach

did not travel at more than ten miles an hour. It was different from a road coach because the horse could be harnessed at either end, and the wheels were smaller. Have you noticed the seat for the guard? The twelve-mile journey cost 1s. 6d. inside and 1s. outside.

When you think how strange these early railway coaches look to us, you must remember that the men who planned them were making something new and had only the road coaches to copy.

In the early coach for the Liverpool and Manchester

Railway on page 59, notice how the shape of the road coach is still kept. The racks on top are for the luggage, as the Directors decided all the passengers should travel inside. Do you think this is a good place for the luggage? Why do you think there are no outside racks on modern trains?

On these two pages are some trains as they ran between Liverpool and Manchester in the 1830's. There are first-class, second-class and third-class carriages. And have you noticed the guard still carries a horn as on the stage coaches?

As the coal mines were opened up farther from the coast, so the lines became longer and set new problems for the engineers, for the line could not always be kept on the level, or down a smooth slope, like this:

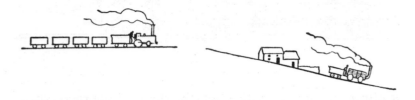

The line sometimes crossed country like this:

Here in one part it was uphill. There were two ways of drawing the trucks up a slope. A stationary engine was built at the top of the slope and pulled the trucks up on ropes. Or else horses were used. You will find a picture of a stationary engine on page 19. Sometimes extra horses waited to be harnessed to the trucks, pulled them to the top of the hill and then were led by a man or boy back again; sometimes the extra horse rode behind the trucks in a cart called a 'dandy' cart and came out when the trucks reached the slope. Writers say that the horses knew their work so well that they walked in and out of the cart of their own accord.

"Dandy" Cart

All these ways of getting the trucks up the hill were slow and expensive, so gradually another way was found. Engineers made the track slope downhill gradually all the way by filling in the valleys or cutting through the hills. Very often the earth taken from a cutting was used to fill in a valley. If the valley was very deep, a viaduct or bridge was built, as the next diagram will show you. The first line to do these things was in Durham where the Causey Arch was built in 1732 and is still standing to-day.

Did you notice that, in both accounts of the opening of the Liverpool and Manchester Railway in the story, the writers thought they would find the flat railway tracks dull? But they found embankments and cuttings just as interesting as hilly roads.

Not all railways were able to follow as flat a route as the Liverpool and Manchester, and the next important railway to be built was the London and Birmingham which gave some difficult problems to the engineer, Robert Stephenson, the son of George Stephenson. The line crossed several flat districts which were separated from one another by ridges of hills. The railway was to pass through the hills by cuttings or tunnels and the earth taken away was to be used to make embankments over the flat districts to make a nearly level track all the way. Here are pictures describing the building of these.

The Tring Cutting

64

THE TRING CUTTING went through the chalk hills north-west of London. It was 2½ miles long and about 40–50 feet deep. One and a half million cubic yards of earth were lifted out and deposited. There were 30–40 horse runs working at a time. You can see these in the picture opposite.

The wheelbarrow was filled at the bottom of the plank. A rope was attached to the front, the man held the handles, the horses were led sideways and the man and the barrow were pulled up, the man keeping the wheel of the barrow on the plank. The man was lying right back as he went up. If the horse did not walk evenly the rope was jerked and the man and the barrow thrown over. The material from one end was carried on to build the WOLVERTON EMBANKMENT, which was 1½ miles long across the Ouse Valley.

In this picture you can see the embankment advancing across the valley. You can see how the lines are laid as it advances and trucks of earth are tipped over the end. The farm has got a great hill before its doors.

65

THE BLISWORTH CUTTING was $1\frac{1}{2}$ miles long and 65 feet deep. One million cubic yards of earth were removed, a third of it solid rock which had to be blasted out. Twenty-five barrels of gunpowder were exploded a week and 3,000 barrels were used in all. It took 800 men and boys more than two years to build. Pumps cleared the water which had collected in the bottom and two locomotives pulled trucks of earth out in addition to that thrown over the sides at the top. In some places the sides were not of rock but of soft clay, and here walls of bricks had to be built to hold them up.

Near CAMDEN TOWN, outside London, brick walls like this were built on concrete. They were slightly curved, as you can see in this picture.

A working shaft in Kilsby Tunnel

KILSBY TUNNEL was the most amazing piece of engineering of the time, for you must remember that it was built by candle and torch light! It was the first long tunnel to be made, 2,423 yards long and 160 feet below the surface. The line had been planned to pass near Northampton but the people there did not wish to have a railway line and forced Stephenson to take the line further away, which meant going through this hill.

When the tunnel was being made the workings were suddenly flooded one afternoon by water from an underground stream and the workmen floated out on a raft! At first there was so much water that everyone thought the tunnel would have to be abandoned but the two Stephensons managed to pump out all the water. It took eight months to do. Then as the tunnel went into the hillside, the walls and roof were bricked in to prevent any more water from the rocks above getting in.

Later engineers were able to do more wonderful things, such as this great bridge of Brunel which he built across the Tamar estuary to carry the Great Western Railway line westwards from Plymouth to Truro.

Saltash Bridge across the River Tamar

Signalling

We have not said anything about signalling yet. Do you remember how Uncle John had said you could not say when a train would arrive because there might be a cow on the line which would delay the train? Do not think that the trains ran along without knowing what was ahead. You will remember that the people thought these engines which moved at 10, 15 or 20 miles an hour were very dangerous and from the beginning they had a form of signalling. Here is a description of it in 1830:

> Throughout the journey travellers will see a number of policemen along the railway who have the important duty of keeping the railway line free from obstruction and making signals as the train passes. Each policeman has two signal flags, one red, the other white: the white flag is held out when no obstruction exists.

How do you think this would work? Does this diagram help you?

Does it make any difference if the train is travelling at 60 miles an hour?

At night each train carried a lamp at the back, which could be turned to shine red or blue. "As long as the train is moving," says a guide-book of 1833, "the red light

69

shows itself to whatever follows, but at the instant of stopping the blue light is turned outward by the guard."

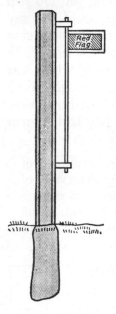

The guide-book then says that "the fire of the engine is sufficient to give warning to the policemen of the approach of a train."

Look at the picture of one of the posts which was erected in 1838. The flag-like piece was turned parallel to the track when the line was clear and across the track when it was blocked. This post replaced the flag although a man was still needed on the spot to turn the board; but you can see that the modern signal was on the way.

Look back at the diagram on the previous page. What was needed to improve on this? Surely, some way of sending a message more quickly than a man could carry it, because now the engines were moving faster than a man or a horse. That is why the invention of the Telegraph was so important to the railways.

The Telegraph is Invented

It would take too long here to explain in detail how the telegraph was invented and works. If you are interested, you will be able to find out more about it from books in your library; but here are some of the most important steps and how they were used by the railways.

1727 Gray and Wheeler discovered that electricity could be sent along a wire.

1753 A suggestion that there should be a wire for each letter of the alphabet and the current should be sent along the wires to make up the words of the message. But it was difficult to receive a message when there were 26 wires to watch and more if numbers were to be included. There were various suggestions to make the receiving easier, such as having the wires in a bath of water and watching bubbles rise from the wires in use, or the receiver having the wires attached to his fingers and noting where he was receiving shocks.

1819 It was discovered that a needle could be moved over a disc on which the letters could be placed. Cooke and Wheatstone worked to improve this in England.

1837 They patented instruments to use on the railway, where there was a great need of sending messages as the trains were travelling faster. The wires were set up first between Camden Town and Euston railway stations. Everyone went along expecting to see the paper carrying the message running along the wires and were very disappointed when they found there was nothing to see unless you were in the signal boxes. Like all new inventions, the instruments would not work at once and even when they were going well at the sending end, there was no reply from the other station. The sender was very bothered until at last there was a message from the other end, "I'm sorry. Asleep by the fire!" However, the telegraph proved a success and was set up next between Paddington and Slough.

An American, Samuel Morse, invented a receiving instrument which held a pencil and made marks on a cylinder of paper attached to a revolving drum. He knew that the letters were too complicated for a machine to form, so he invented a code of dots and dashes which bears his name. Later he found the pencil was not very good and a metal bar for tapping out the dots and dashes was used instead.

1845 A murderer escaping by train was caught because of a message sent ahead of the train by telegraph. The message said: "A murder has just been committed at Salthill and the suspected murderer was seen to take a first-class ticket for London by the train which left Slough at 7.42 p.m. He is in the garb of a Quaker with a brown great coat on, which reaches nearly down to his feet; he is in the last compartment of the second first-class carriage." The police were ready at London to follow the man and later to arrest him. Everyone was amazed how easily it had been done by telegraph.

To-day the telegraph is much more complicated than this because many more improvements have been made which would take too long to explain here. Even pictures can be sent nowadays! How different from 1837 when the chief uses of the telegraph were said to be:

1. To stop a runaway train!
2. To tell the ticket collector at the next station about the gentleman with the second-class ticket sitting in a first-class carriage!

— ·· | ·· | ··· — | · | · — · | — || · — | · — ·· | · — ·· ||
— | · — · | · — | ·· | — · | ··· || · — · — · — ||
·· — · | · — ·· | — — — | — — — | — ·· | ··· ||
··· | · — — | · | · — — · | — || · — | · — — | · — | — · — ·· ||
— ··· | · — · | ·· | — ·· | — — · | · ||

72

Stations

It was quite new to have a building where passengers could wait and could buy their tickets, where luggage could be collected and the railway staff shelter. When the stage coaches had started more than a hundred years earlier, they had stopped outside the public inns which had always given shelter, food and drink to travellers. At first the stations were wooden shelters rather like a cattle or wagon shed on a farm to-day, but gradually the engineers found out the type of building they needed and asked the architects to plan it. Most of the large towns where many people used the station had a shed big enough to cover the tracks as well as the platforms and joined to the station building at one end. To make the station as light as possible, glass was used in the roof. Here is a picture of Liverpool Station:

On the smaller stations there was only a small area of shelter on the platform. Here the architects met a difficulty, for an ordinary lean-to roof on the station building was not possible, as the posts holding it up got in the way of the doors of the train. So the posts had to be set back from the edge of the platform. There were many ways of doing this and, as they were built of wood, cast-iron, or glass, nearly every station in the country was different. Have a look at the stations near your home. Notice all the various shapes in the iron or wood work of the roof.

Here are four different ways of holding up these shelters, or verandas as they were first called. Can you say how architects solved the problem of where to put the posts?

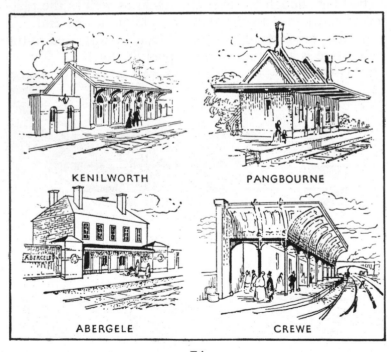

KENILWORTH   PANGBOURNE

ABERGELE   CREWE

The railway builders made grand fronts to their stations because they wanted to show how up to date they were and they wished to celebrate the building of the railway. Some of them were copied from other buildings, as these pictures will show.

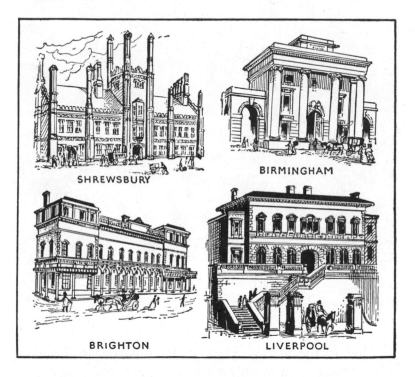

SHREWSBURY

BIRMINGHAM

BRIGHTON

LIVERPOOL

At first platforms were called parades. The smaller stations did not have them at first, as you can see in the picture on page 57, but later they were built at all stations so that the passengers did not have such a climb into the carriages and also did not wait for the train on a wet or muddy piece of ground.

This picture shows you what it was like at a railway station in 1843.

This is the station yard at Paddington in London, where the road and railway meet. The train is on top of the arches. What a bustle there is in the yard! Do you see all the different means of transport?

Opposite is a scene in 1837 at Euston Station, London. You can still see the same roof and pillars on Platform 6 of this station to-day. What wouldn't you see if you visited this station to-day?

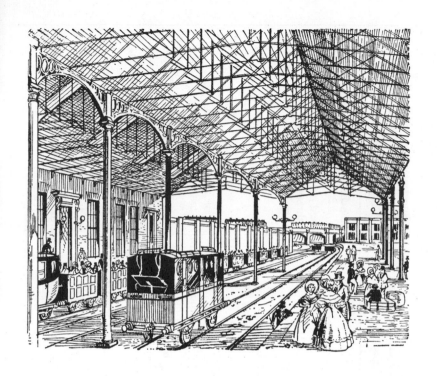

The Railway Timetable

To-day, when anyone wants to look up the time of a train, he calls for a railway timetable called "Bradshaw." Did you know this was called after GEORGE BRADSHAW (1801–1853), who was born at Pendleton, near Manchester? He was apprenticed in Manchester and later set up on his own as a printer and engraver of pictures and maps.

In 1839 he published the first set of railway timetables and in 1840 he changed its name to "Bradshaw's Railway Companion." From December 1841 this was published monthly to keep it up to date.

Secretary and Treasurer:
H. Booth, Liverpool and Manchester
Engineer: E. Woods, Liverpool

Superintendents of Goods:
A. Comber, Liverpool
J. Green, Manchester

Liverpool to Manchester

1st class trains	2nd only through trains	1st and 2nd class Road trains	3rd class road trains
8NU am	....	7.15 am	6.45 am
8.45 am	....	10.30 am	....
10¼NU am	....	....	12½ nn*
11.45 am	....	....	5½ pm through 5.0 pm
2.0 pm	1.30NU pm	2.30 pm	6.30 pm
4.15 pm	3.35NU pm	5.30 pm	....
....	6NU pm	7.45 pm*	....

Manchester to Liverpool

1st class trains	2nd only through trains	1st and 2nd class road trains	3rd class road trains
8¼NU am	....	....	6½ am
9.0 am	....	7.15 am	....
10½NU am	....	11.15 am	10.0 am*
12.15 nn	....	....	....
2.0 pm	1.30NU pm	2.45 pm	....
....	3.50NU pm	5.30 pm	5½ pm through
....	6¼NU pm	8.20 pm*	6½ pm

*Stopping at Huyton Gate, Rainhill, St. Helen's Junction, Newton, Parkside, Kenyon Junction, Bury Lane and Patricroft.

NU By the trains marked NU being especially North Union Trains, the passengers for Manchester and Liverpool will be detained unavoidably at Parkside till the arrival of the trains from Preston.

Fares: By the first class carriages, four inside, royal mail 6/6; six inside, glass coach, 4/0; third class 2/6.

Passengers by first class trains may take a ticket entitling them to be conveyed to Liverpool or Manchester and back the same day for 10s.

Children under 12 years, half price; in the arms, under 4 years, free.

Let us examine a copy of the book which James had. There is a copy which you can see in the library in Manchester. Perhaps your library has one too.

The Railway Companion, August 1st, 1845

It is a small book, measuring $2\frac{1}{2}$ by $4\frac{1}{2}$ inches, with stiff green covers and containing 72 pages. It has other details besides the timetables of the railways. This is what is printed on the title page:

> The Times of Departure, Fares of the Railways of Great Britain and Ireland, also the Hackney Coach Fares from the Principal Stations. Illustrated with maps of the country through which the Railways pass, and plans of London, Birmingham, Bristol, Liverpool and Manchester.

On the first page are General Instructions for Railway Travellers. Here are some of them:

> The doors are closed at the precise time for starting the Trains and Passengers should be at the Stations at least 10 minutes before the time of departure.
>
> Post Horses may be readily obtained at each *terminus*.
>
> Dogs are conveyed at a small charge in a proper carriage but are not allowed to be taken inside the carriages.
>
> Smoking is not allowed at the Stations, nor in any of the carriages.

On the opposite page you can see what James was looking at, to find the time of the train for his Uncle. It gives the times of the trains on the Liverpool and Manchester Railway.

What People Wrote about Railways

You will understand that there were always those who wanted railways and those who did not. If you have a discussion in class on any subject there will always be some in favour and some against the motion. For the most part, however, there were more people writing against railways before 1835 and more writing in favour of them after that date. First let us consider the reasons put forward against the railways.

Against the Railways:

The landowners did not want a railway running across their land cutting it into two, even if the railway company did build bridges over the line. Sometimes the railway was planned to go in front of their house. Here is a picture made by a Mr. Cookson of Durham to show how the railway would spoil the view from his house which you can see peeping over the top of the embankment. You can understand that he did not want to see this mound of earth instead of the fields and trees. The House of Commons were so sorry for him that they ordered the railway line to take another route.

Some of the landowners were very keen huntsmen and one line was nearly stopped because it would spoil the hunting of one of the Peers.

The newspaper JOHN BULL said in 1835:

The whole face of the kingdom is to be tattooed with these horrid things—huge mounds are to cut up our beautiful valleys; the noise and smell of locomotive steam-engines are to disturb the quiet of the farmer and gentleman.

You will think that some people opposed the railways for strange reasons. There were some who said that the noise would upset the cows and hens and mean that the country would be short of milk and eggs! Have you ever been past a field of cows grazing? They do not often look at the train but carry on with their eating, yet everyone laughed when Stephenson said that this was so. Then the doctors said that the noise would be bad for the travellers' nerves, or that they would catch colds in the tunnels (but some doctors said that the shaking would help the digestion, so you see there was something to be said in favour after all!).

Some people disliked going through a tunnel because they imagined that they would die either from lack of fresh air or from a fall of roof. When the Box Tunnel ($1\frac{3}{4}$ miles long) was opened in 1841 on the Great Western line between London and Bath, many people travelled by stage coach between Box and Corsham, the stations at either end of the tunnel!

Of course, the people who collected the turnpike tolls or who owned stage coaches and coaching inns or stables, or made saddles and harness, all thought they would be ruined. Many of them did lose money on account of the railways, especially where the railway line did not come near a town which had been on an important coach route.

For the Railways:

Once the railways had been built people began to praise them. There were funny verses printed and serious books written; here are some of them:

> If you will listen to my song
> I'll not detain you long.
> On the 1st of May the folks did throng
> To view the Oxford railway.
> To have a ride—what a treat—
> Father, mother, son and daughter
> Along the line like one o'clock
> By fire, and steam and water.
>
> *Chorus:* Rifum, Tifum, mirth and fun.
> Don't you wonder how it's done?
> Carriages without horses run
> On the Hampton and Oxford Railway.

The railway is most glorious and delightful travelling. I went in the first class, being farthest from the engine, much more comfortable and built like a coach. Five of them, one behind the other, started at the rate of a trotting horse, then faster and faster, until it goes at the rate of ten miles an hour over the top of the houses up to the first station, then on with hills on either side. (Leigh Hunt to his parents, 1840.)

> First the shrill whistle, then the distant roar,
> The ascending cloud of steam, the gleaming brass,
> The mighty moving arm; and on again
> The mass comes thundering like an avalanche o'er
> The quaking earth; a thousand faces pass—
> A moment, and are gone, like whirlwind sprites,
> Scarce seen . . .

The most famous artist of the day, William Turner, painted a picture in 1844 which he called "Wind, Rain and Steam." The train comes on through a storm of wind and rain, the light from the firebox lighting up the dark clouds above.

There were those, of course, who were very impressed with the way the railway improved trade and farming.

A gentleman went to Liverpool in the morning, purchased and took back with him to Manchester 150 tons of cotton, which he sold and afterwards obtained an offer for a similar quantity. He went again; and actually, that same evening, delivered the second quantity in Manchester, having travelled 120 miles in four separate journeys, and bought, sold and delivered, thirty miles off, at two distinct deliveries, 300 tons of goods in about 12 hours. The feat is perfectly astounding; and, had it been hinted at 50 years ago, would have been said to be impossible.

The improvement of the farm land impressed many.

Chat Moss is now being farmed beside the Liverpool and Manchester Railway and entirely because of the railway. A stranger to-day cannot imagine how barren and lonely this land was before the coming of the railway. The traveller by the railway can now see, in the very middle of this great bog, well cultivated and neatly arranged fields, crops of oats, wheat and potatoes, farm house and cottages built, the ploughman working, trees growing well where a few years ago it was all loneliness and silence.

On page 14 of the story, Mr. Kennedy talked about the opponents of the Liverpool and Manchester Railway arguing every line of the Bill. Here is some of the evidence given in 1834 when the Great Western Railway Bill (for a line from London to Bristol) was being considered in Parliament. Charles Walker, the Mayor of Bristol, was asked:

Are you in trade?
Yes.

In what line?

A large wholesale brass concern.

Have you been in the habit of sending goods to London?

Yes, from 150 to 200 tons.

How have you generally sent them?

By inland waterway. [Canal]

Has your business suffered by delay and uncertainty?

Yes, last winter for two or three weeks we could not send anything because of the floods on the River Avon.

Mr. William Reed was called.

You are Secretary to the Manchester Agricultural Society? Yes.

Do you know anything of the Liverpool and Manchester Railway?

Yes, I lived on a farm through which it passes for three or four years and now live within a very short distance of it.

What sort of agricultural produce is carried by it?

Pigs, eggs, bacon, butter, hay, clover in a green state for the horses at either end, corn of all descriptions, potatoes; in fact almost every variety.

Do they also carry manure and lime? Yes.

Mr. Joseph Locke was called.

You are an engineer living in Liverpool? Yes.

What is the rate of travelling on the railway? Twenty miles an hour.

Can you count upon the time of your arrival? To a few minutes.

Why do people travel by railway?

For cheapness, saving of time and for ease and comfort.

The mail is carried three or four times a day between the towns?

Yes.

84

Railway Mania

This is how we describe the mad way in which many people acted between 1844 and 1849.

As you read in the story, the men who decided to build a railway line—like the ones who met in Liverpool in 1824—drew up a prospectus on which they put all the advantages for building a line and, as they were trying to persuade other people to lend them money, they made it sound as pleasant as possible. They tried to persuade people with money that if they bought railway shares they would get rich much more quickly than by any other way. This table shows the traffic and profits of the Liverpool and Manchester Railway during the first years.

Year	Passengers	Profit	Goods in tons	Profit
1831	445,047	£56,918	108,180	£23,696
1832	356,945	£37,463	159,443	£20,635
1833	386,492	£46,723	194,704	£139,881

You have seen how the Liverpool and Manchester Railway was a great success, so everyone thought that every other railway would be too. But many of the lines did not run between such large towns as Liverpool and Manchester nor where there was such a lot of travelling and so they were not all successful. Some people, when they found that they were not getting the profits they had expected, sold their shares cheaply. It was in this way that a linen-draper of York, George Hudson, was able to buy up many thousands of shares in railways in the Midlands and North-east of England during 1840 and 1841 until he controlled many hundreds of miles of line. He did not act very honestly but, so long as the shareholders gained some profits, they did not ask how they had been obtained. In 1842 business improved and because of all the shares he held, Hudson became a very important man in the railway world. He wanted to see more lines built and worked hard to persuade more people to lend money for this purpose.

Parliament, which had opposed the early railways, now welcomed them. Everyone in the country thought that more railways would make the country rich; few thought as Stephenson did that there were not the men or machines to make and run them. Thus in 1845 Parliament allowed the building of 2,883 miles of new line, and in 1846, 4,790 miles. For several years Hudson had it all his own way. He was known as the Railway King, and in 1845 even PUNCH published a cartoon of him which you can see on the opposite page. Just as the Queen holds a reception or levee, so the PUNCH cartoonist, Leech, showed Hudson holding his. Here is a remark in the RAILWAY TIMES of September 1843 by a man who doubted that Hudson should be so powerful:

> I consider Mr. Hudson a shrewd, honest man, but for pity's sake, sir, call the attention of the shareholders to the power this person is obtaining. Shareholders should be careful before they raise a railway autocrat, with power greater than the Prime Minister.

Gladstone tried to check his power in 1844 but it was useless, until Hudson could wangle the accounts no longer.

Hudson had been paying profits to people from the money other people lent him for investing in new lines. But when he built no new lines people began to ask questions. At a meeting at York, Hudson failed to answer correctly, then became confused, and immediately people thought there was something strange. Committees were set up to examine the matter and all his dishonest actions were seen. The Railway Mania was at an end. Hudson went to France and became a very poor man and hundreds of people lost all their money, for very few lines of railway had been built by him.

Hudson's Levée, by Leech of *Punch*
(*Reproduced by permission of the Proprietors of* Punch)

Results of having Railways across the Country

It was not easy for Mr. Kennedy and James to see all the results of the new railways. Here are some of them:

Travel was cheaper and quicker, so people journeyed about the country who had not done so in the days of stage coaches. Families could keep in touch with their relations, people were able to see that the folks who lived at the other end of the kingdom were not very different from themselves. The increased speeds meant that papers, magazines and letters and therefore ideas travelled much more quickly than before. There had been a marked difference between the north and south, east and west, town and country in the eighteenth century, but this was no longer true by the second half of the nineteenth century.

87

There was a change in government too when Members of Parliament were only a few hours from their constituencies. The people could now keep a watch on what their Member did and said in the House and could easily visit him to state their point of view.

Trade was helped both within the country and at the docks. The food of the country changed when country produce could be carried more easily into the towns without growing stale.

The railway companies became the greatest employers of labour, thousands of people working on the different kinds of jobs you find to-day. New towns grew up. Perhaps the most famous of all railway towns is Crewe, which grew from a tiny village into the huge collection of railway works, shops, houses and other buildings you find to-day. Swindon is another railway town.

Notice that the railways were a complete monopoly, that is, no one could compete against them, nor force them to make improvements.

Notice too that there was no national plan when the railways were built. A group of men who provided the money decided to build a line between two towns and the engineer and contractor carried this out. Sometimes there was another line being built and sometimes the line was not really needed. Thus to-day Britain has the densest railway network in the world. This was an unexpected advantage during the last war as it was difficult to put the railways out of action by air attack. If one was damaged, there was nearly always another way round. On the continent of Europe, however, it was different, for in many countries there the governments had planned the railways in the nineteenth century and had planned only one route between any two towns.

THINGS TO DO

1. On page 1, 1845 was described as 'the Year of the Railway Mania.' Can you now explain this description?

2. Make a list of the ways by which cotton has travelled from Liverpool to Manchester during the last 200 years. Now make a series of drawings to show these changes.

3. What is a turnpike road? How did it get this name? Who paid tolls? What was done with the money?
There are some toll bridges to-day. Have you one near your home? What are the tolls to-day?

4. Read again the difficulties Stephenson and his assistant Gooch met in making the survey of the line. Write a letter which Thomas Gooch might have sent to a friend describing their experiences.

5. Study the railway from your town to the next. Imagine that you are the engineer planning its construction. What difficulties would you have to overcome? Are there any rivers to cross? or hills to pass through? Make a diagrammatic map and mark these difficulties and write on it how you would overcome them.

6. Do you remember what happened at Parkside on the Opening Day when the engines stopped for water? You can read it again on page 30. Can you write a short play about this? Who would be the characters? What would they be doing and saying?

7. Read again the reasons for and against railways, as set out on pages 80–84. If you had lived in 1830, which side would you have been on? Does everyone in your class agree with you? You could have a debate on this matter.

8. Many of you will know a great deal about the locomotives of to-day, but if you do not, get a book on modern trains from the library and compare them with the early engines in this book.

9. What ways other than steam are there to-day for driving locomotives? Can you make drawings of these engines and write a short description of each? You will need a book from the library.

10. Read again the section on signalling on page 69. How do signals work to-day? Find out about the modern signal box.

11. On page 79 you will find some General Instructions for Railway Travellers in 1845. Can you alter these so that they would do for to-day?

12. In your local library you will find a copy of Bradshaw's Railway Guide for this present year. Find the page giving the time-tables of trains between Liverpool and Manchester. What are the differences between the timetable to-day and the timetable on page 78 of this book?

13. From Bradshaw's Railway Guide, plan the train timetable for a week's holiday around Britain travelling each day to another town. Perhaps you would like to visit six different cathedrals, or you may have relatives in six different towns, or would like to visit six different seaside towns.

14. Study a map showing the railways of Britain. Where is the network thickest? Why is this? Where are there few railways? Would you expect this? Make a map of the railway network around your town, putting in the destination where the lines leave the map. Are there any big junctions near your home? Where are the trains going?

15. Study the station buildings near your home. Make sketches of them. When were they built?

16. Look at the picture on page 76 again. Visit the yard of your station. Make a list of the different means of transport entering it to-day and compare it with a list of those shown on page 76. Draw a picture of the yard to-day.

17. On page 83 you have a short description of a famous picture painted by William Turner. Paint a picture of an exciting moment in the running of a train.

18. Make a list of all the jobs on the railway which you can think of to-day. Which would you like to do? Write down your reasons. Are there any which you would *not* like to do? Why? Are there any jobs which were not done in 1845?

GLOSSARY

This is a list of special words. If the word you want to know is not here, look for it in your dictionary.

axle : the rod on which a wheel revolves.

beam : the lever in an engine connecting *piston* rod and *crank*.

Bill : the first statement of a proposed Act of Parliament.

buffer : springs or padding to lessen a shock.

bull-head : a rail with a thickened top (see picture, page 55).

cast iron : iron which has been heated and poured into a mould of the required shape.

chair : an iron or steel holder for keeping a rail in place (see picture, page 53).

cog-engine : an engine whose wheels have projections which fit into those on a *rack rail*.

Committee Stage : the stage after a Bill has been read in the whole House of Commons when a number of members of Parliament study it in detail clause by clause.

condense : to turn from gas or vapour into liquid.

Corn Laws : laws which stopped the export of corn and put a duty on imported corn in times of shortage.

coupled : fastened together.

crank : a bar fashioned so that it can change a straight in-and-out movement into a circular movement.

cutting : a levelled way through hilly country (see picture, page 63).

cylinder : the part of an engine where steam acts on the *piston*.

drawbar : the bar that bears the couplings by which railway carriages and trucks are connected in a train.

driving wheels : the large wheels of a locomotive which are turned by the engine.

firebox : fuel chamber of a steam boiler.

fish-bellied : a rail curved underneath like a fish's belly (see picture, page 53).

flange : the projecting rim of a wheel or rail (see picture, page 50).

gauge : the standard measurement between railway lines.

gearing : wheels working on one another by teeth.

horsepower : a measure of the rate of doing work.

locomotive : a steam engine for moving on rails.

piston : a closely fitting block that moves backwards and forwards inside a *cylinder*.

plateway : an early railway with *flanged* rails and smooth-wheeled trucks and engines.

prospectus : a circular describing a public enterprise.

rack rail : a rail with projections which fit into those of a *cog*-wheel (see picture, page 53).

safety valve : a device in a steam-boiler to stop it from bursting.

share : one of the equal parts into which a company's capital is divided, giving the holder a proportion of the profits.

shareholder : owner of shares.

sleeper : a timber support for a rail (see picture, page 55).

smokebox : part of the engine placed at the base of the funnel.

staithe : a pier for loading coal into ships (see picture, page 38).

stationary engine : an engine fixed in one place to operate machinery (see picture, page 19).

survey : an examination of a piece of land for a particular purpose.

terminus : the station at the end of a railway line.

trailing wheels : wheels which are not driven by the engine.

turnpike : a gate (often with pikes or spikes on it) set across a road to stop traffic passing until the toll has been paid.

vacuum : a space in which there is no air.

viaduct : a series of arches for carrying a road or railway over a valley (see picture, page 16).

water-crane : machinery for pumping water into an engine.

water-scoop tender : a truck fitted to pick up water for an engine (see picture, page 58).

wrought iron : iron which has been heated and then hammered or rolled into the required shape.